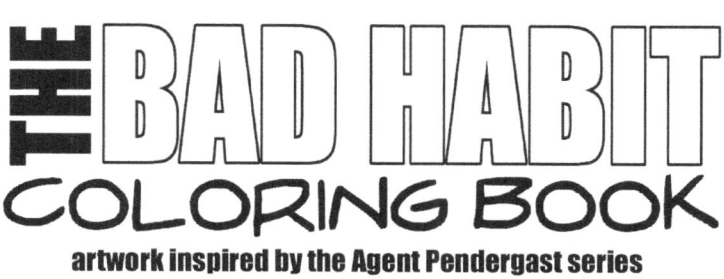

COLORING BOOK

artwork inspired by the Agent Pendergast series
by Douglas Preston and Lincoln Child

Text and Illustrations by Tiffany Stafford

To Team Pendergast,

And to Malcolm. Get your crayons ready.

Author's Note

Even though each design is printed on its own page, I recommend using a scrap piece of paper beneath the page you are coloring. Especially if you are using markers that bleed through. Suggested mediums to use on these pages are colored pencils, conté crayons, pastels, regular crayon, and markers. Water- and oil-based mediums are not recommended.

-Tiffany, August 2015

Table of Contents
(in order of appearance)

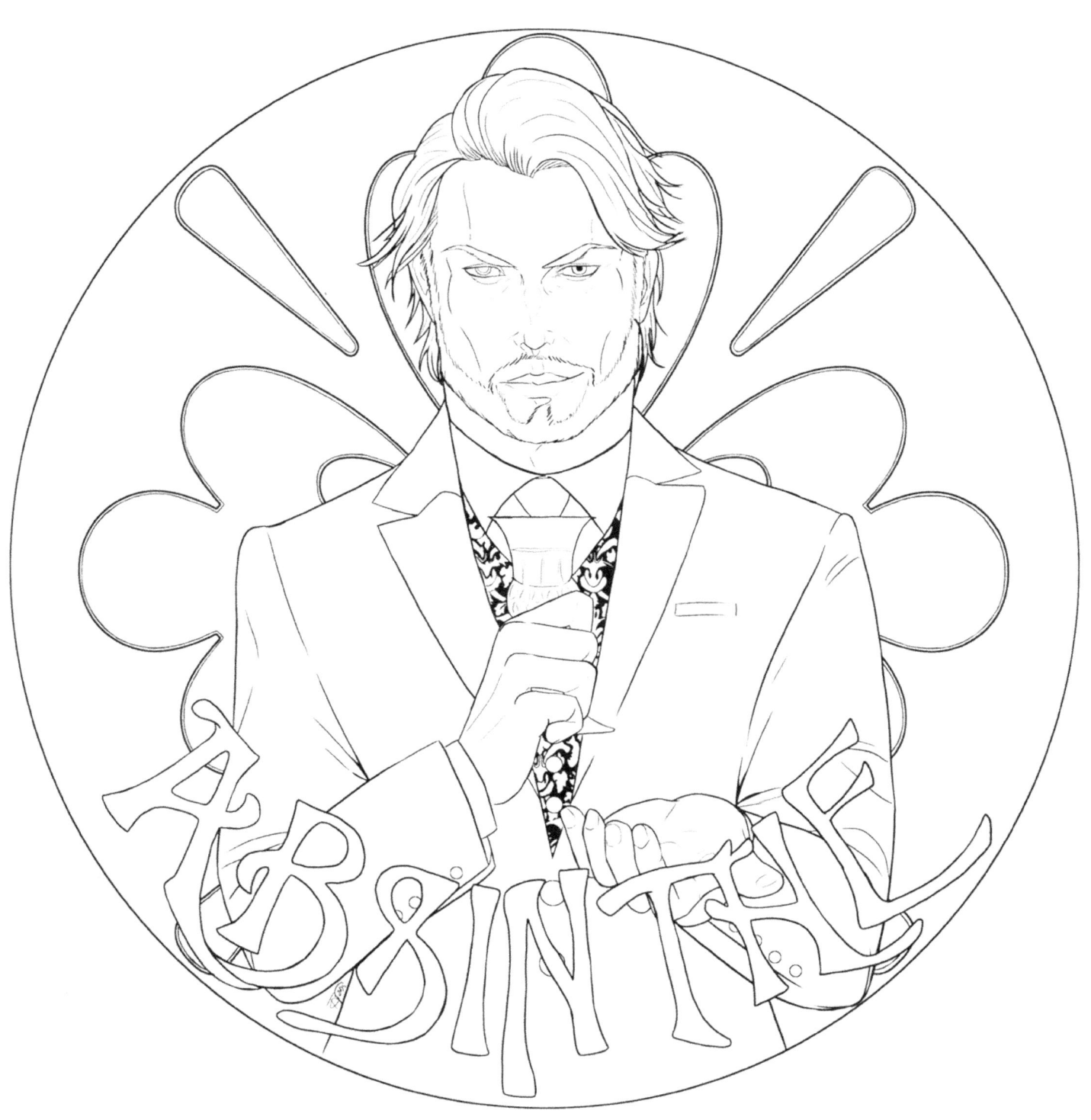

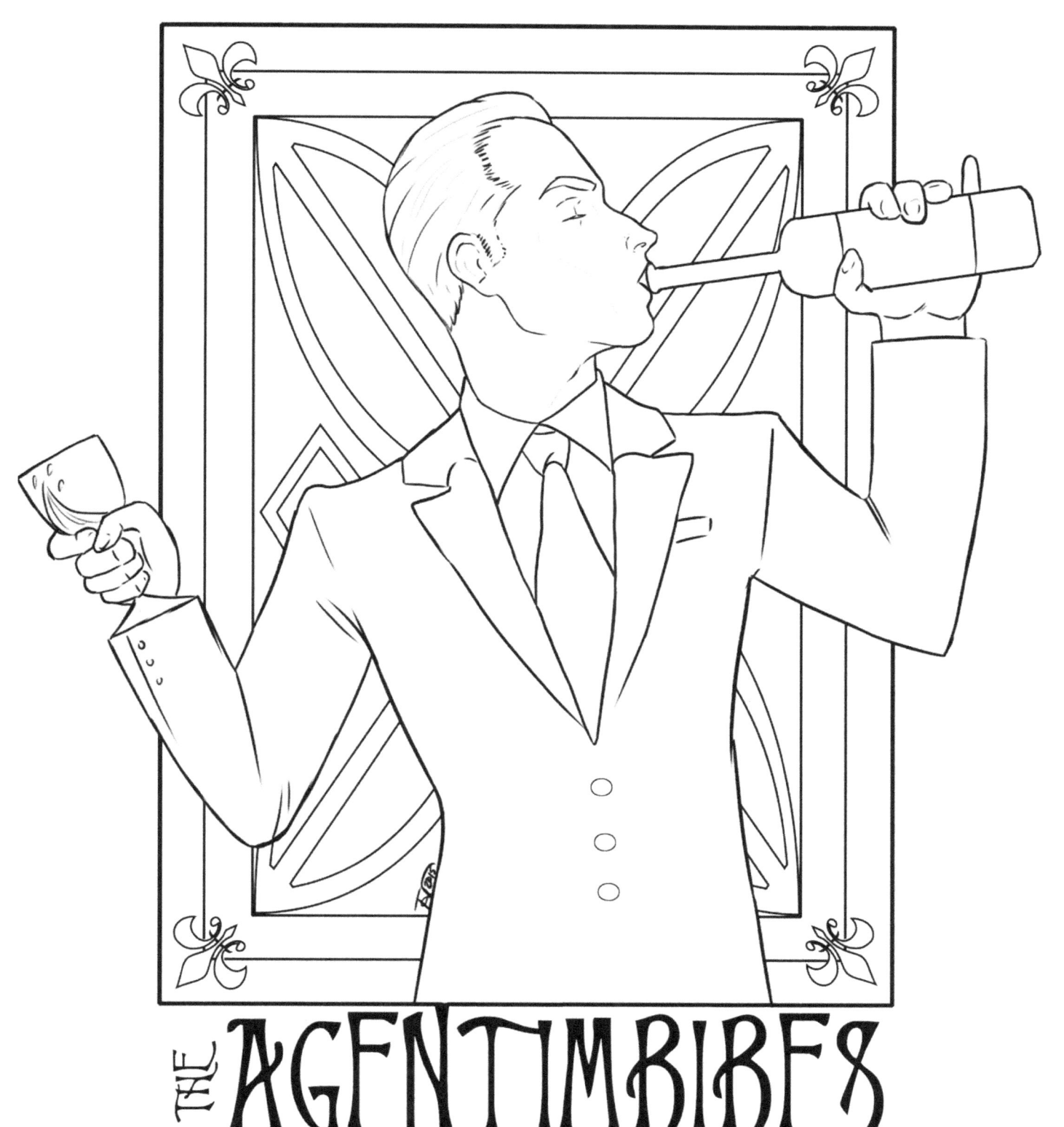

THE AGENTIMBIBES

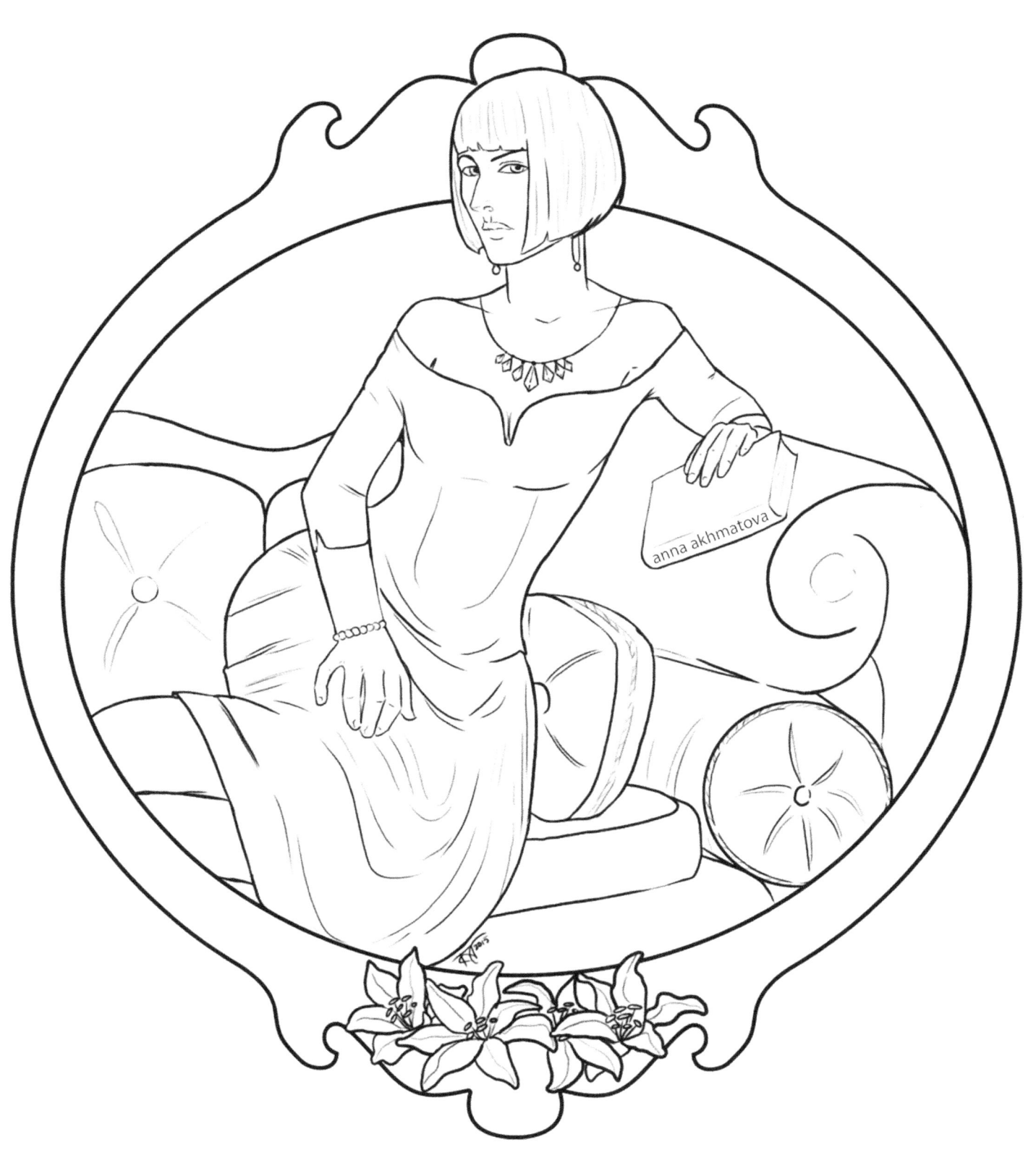

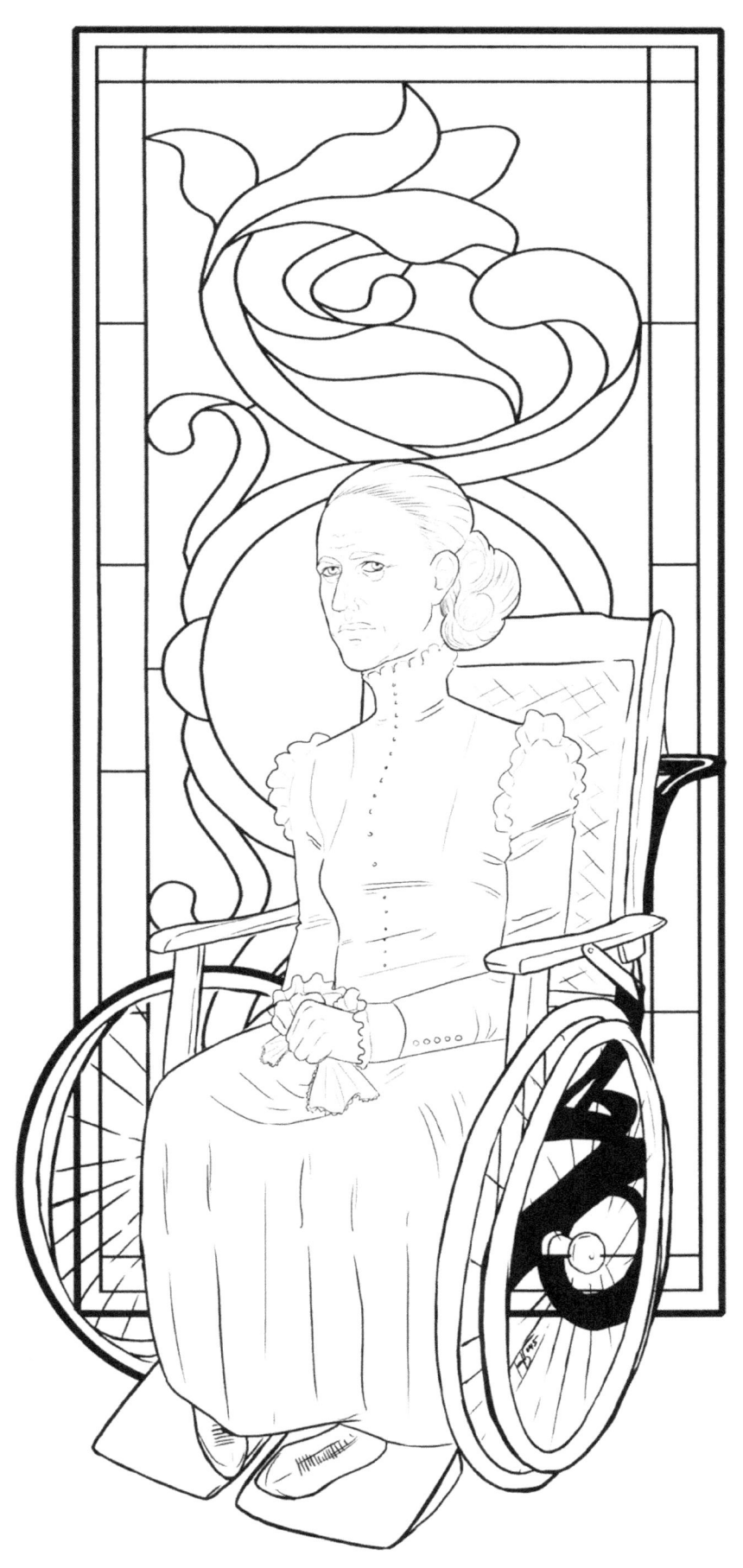

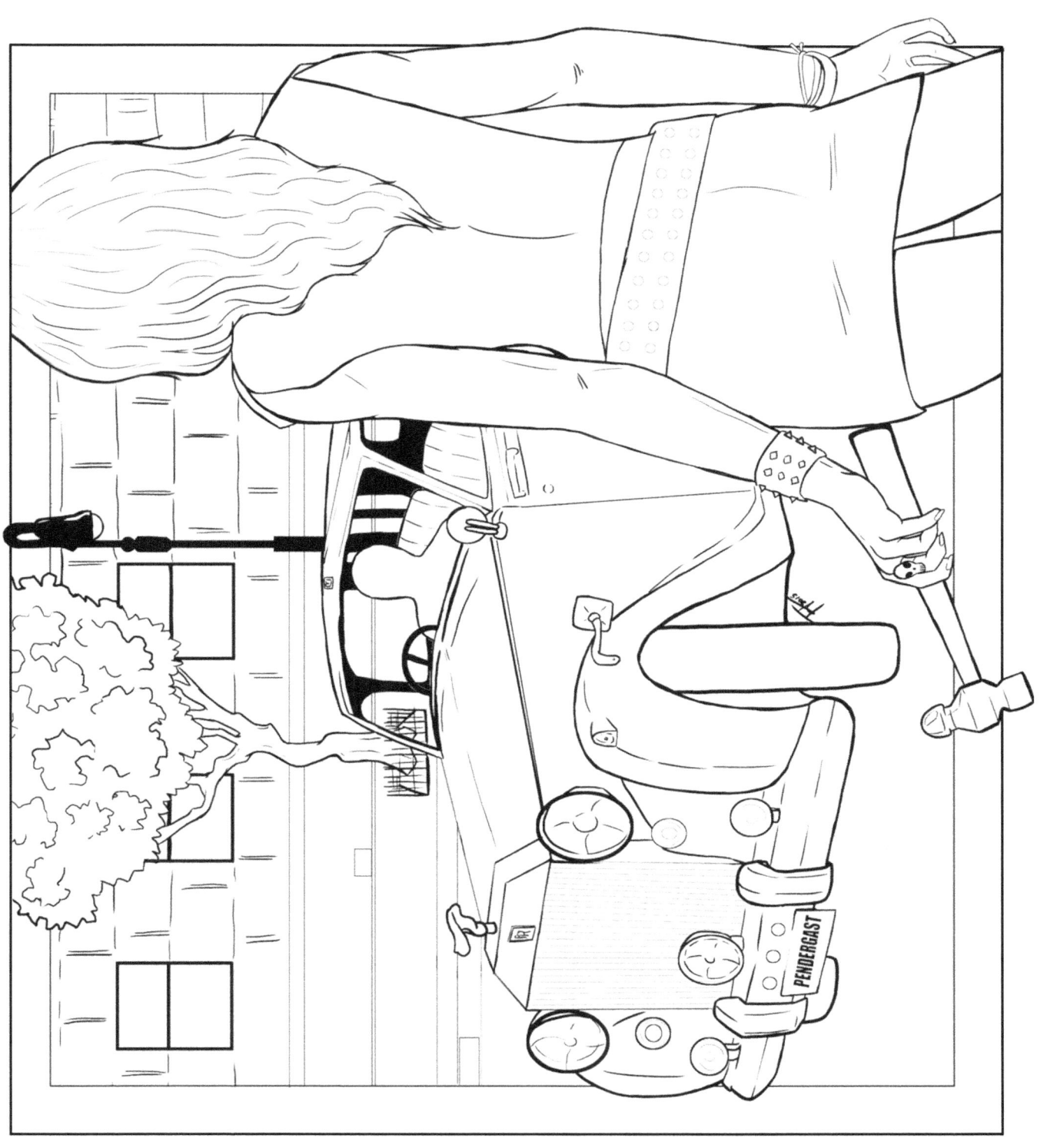

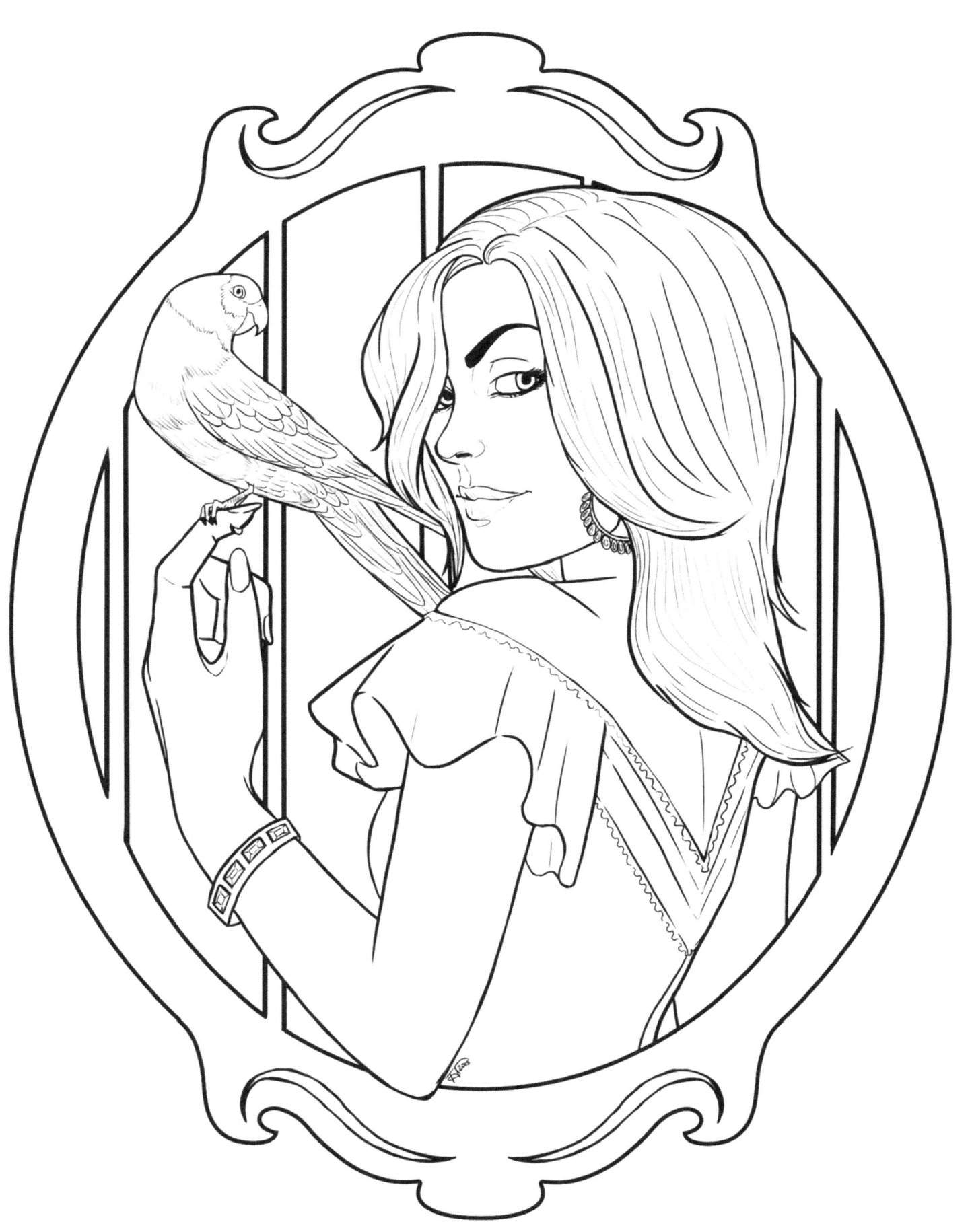

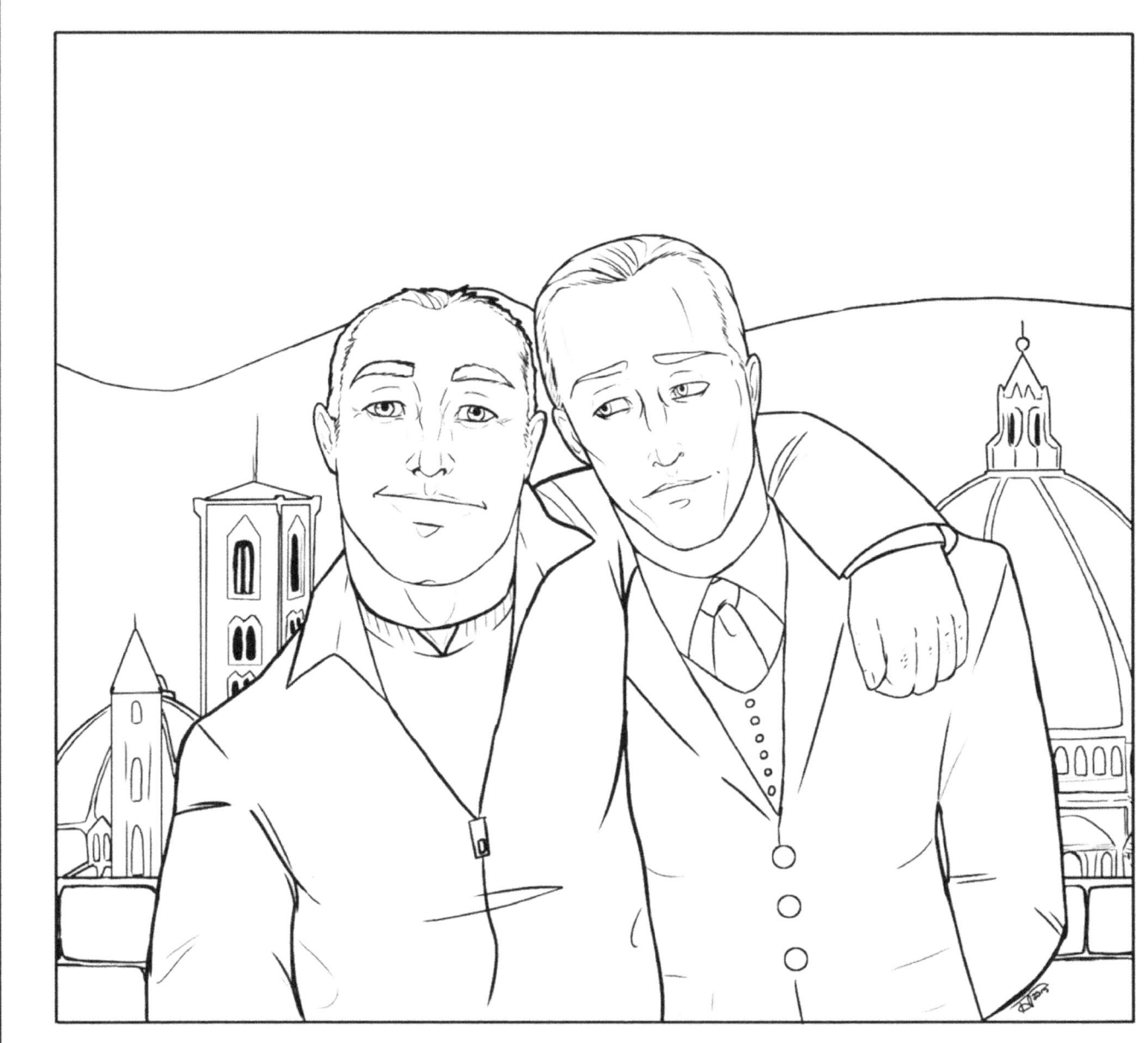

Me and Al, Italy '04

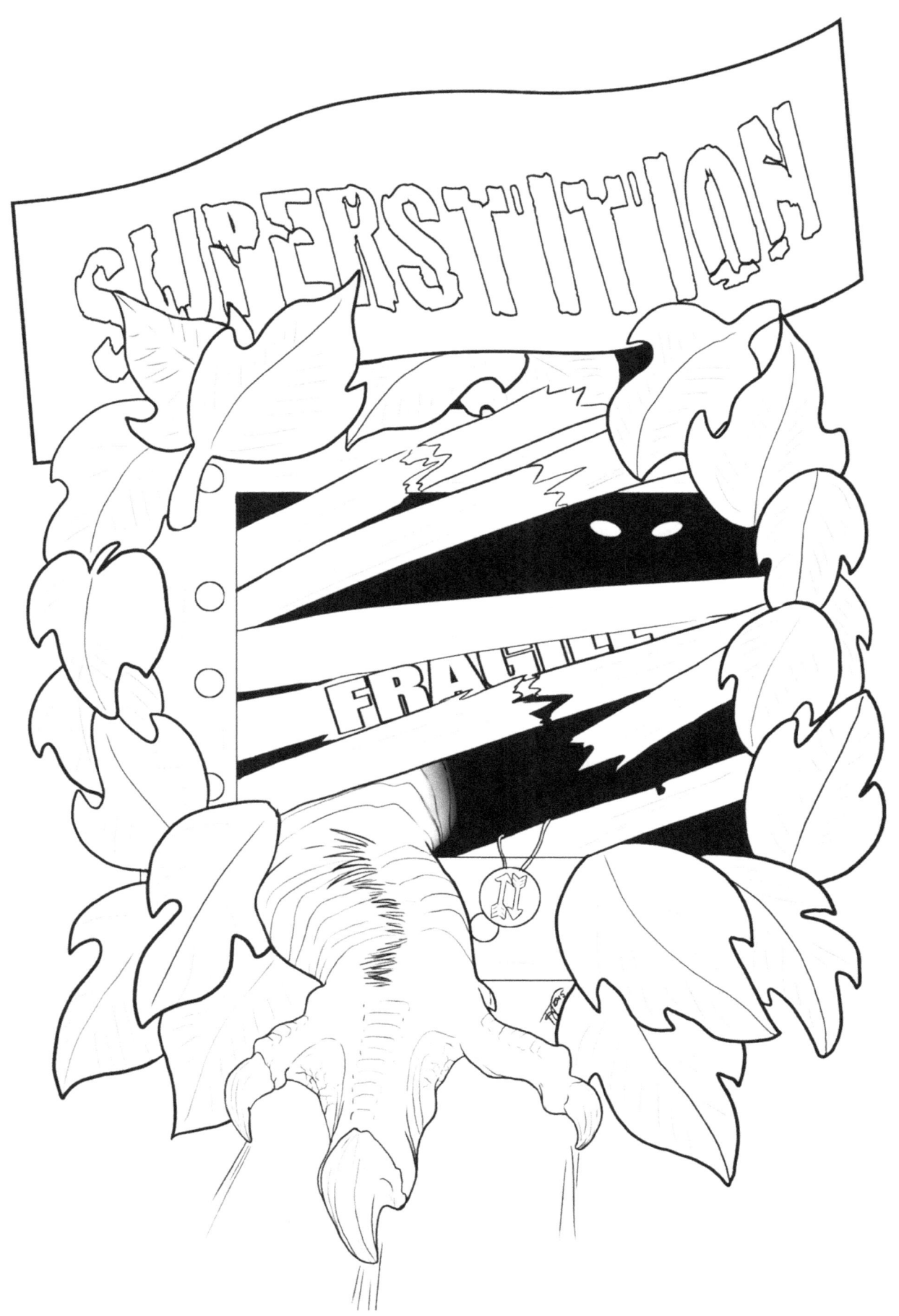

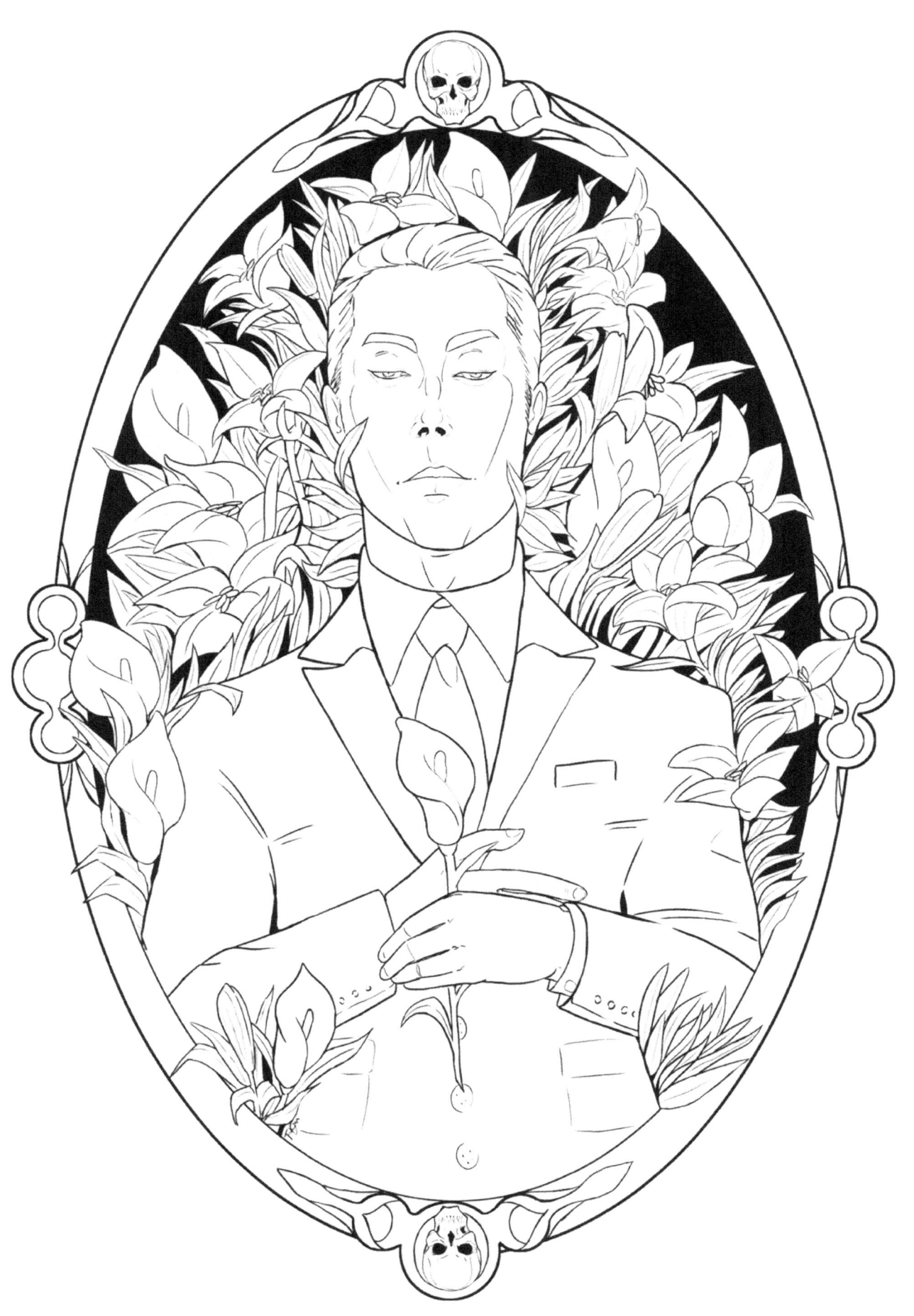

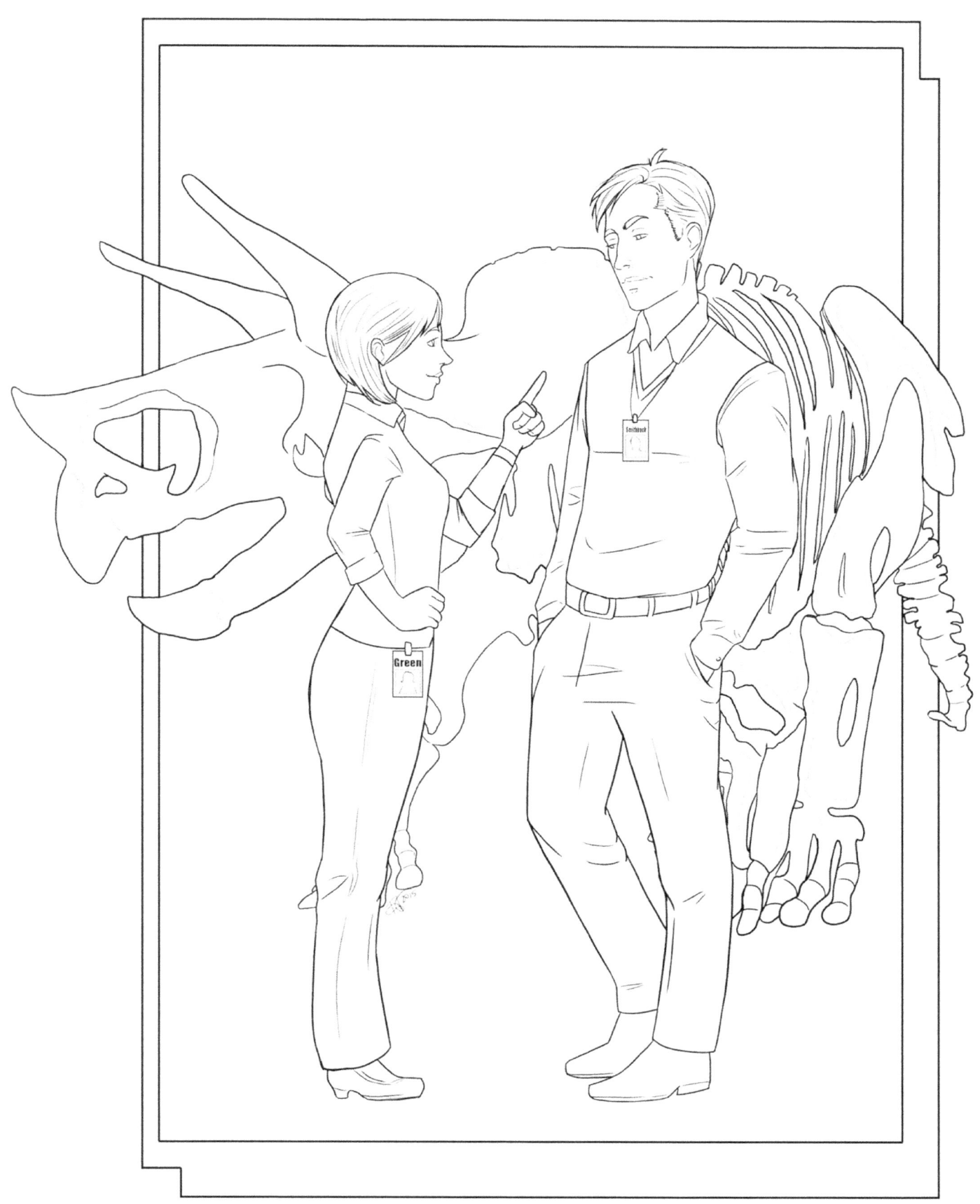

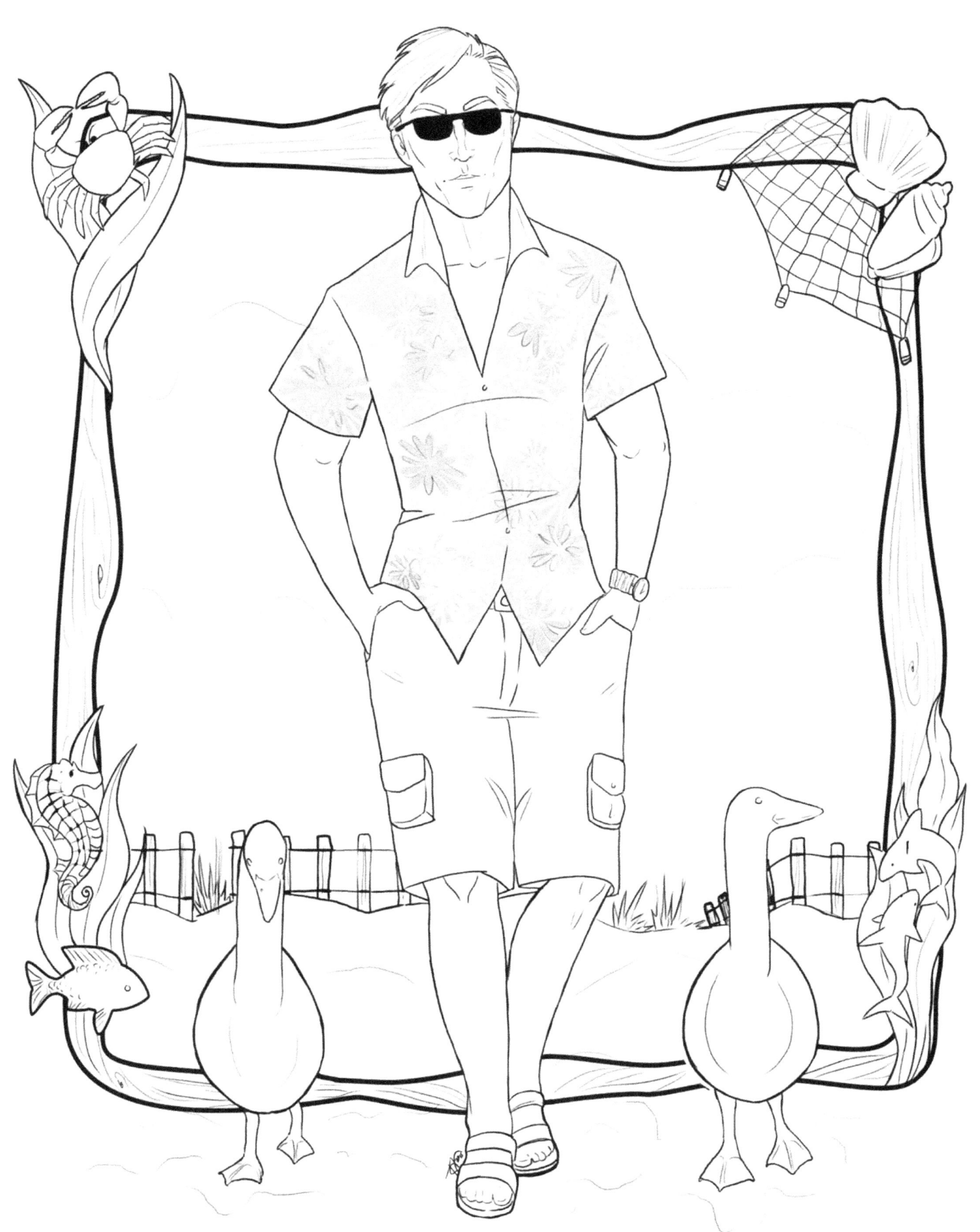

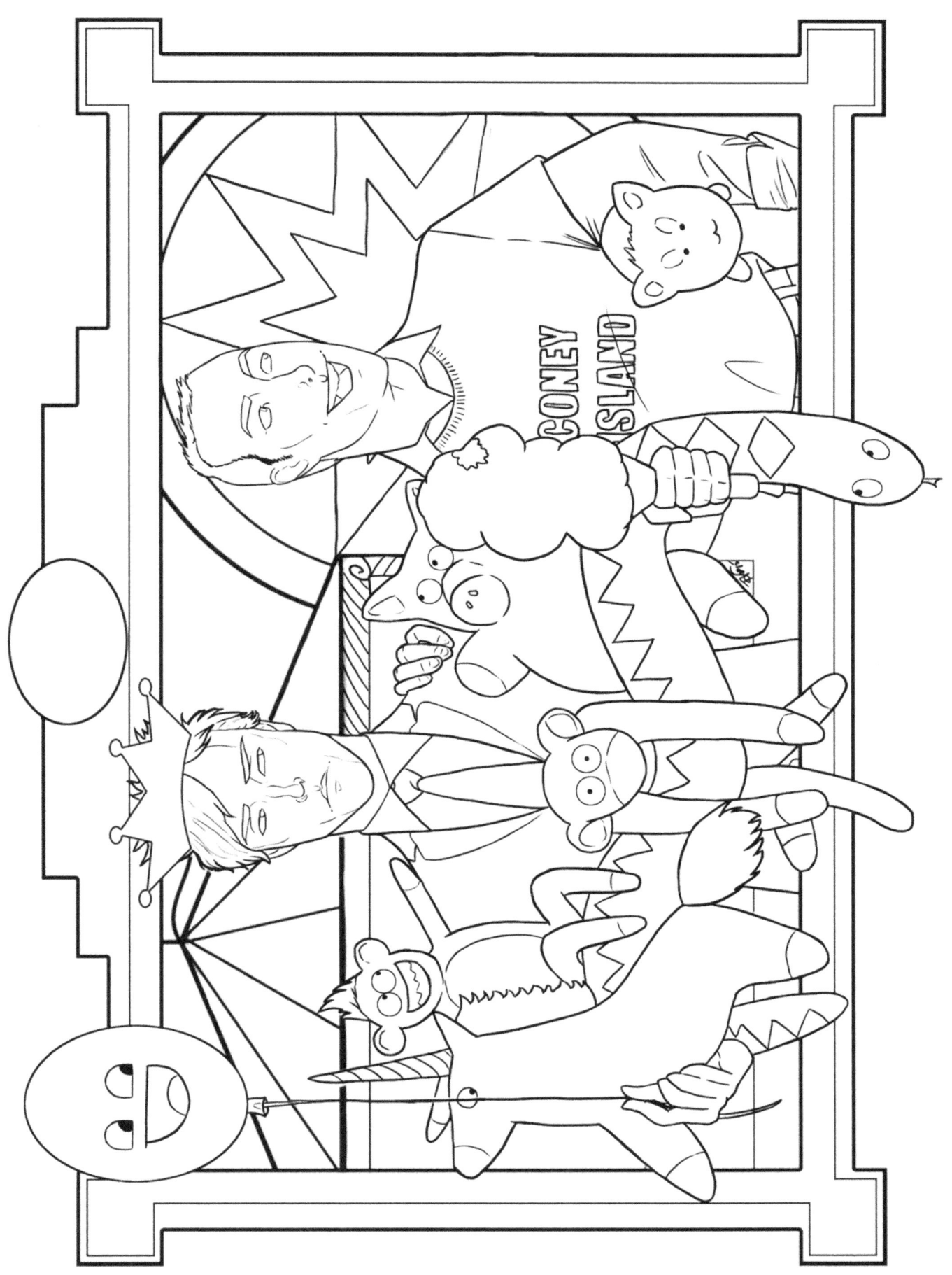

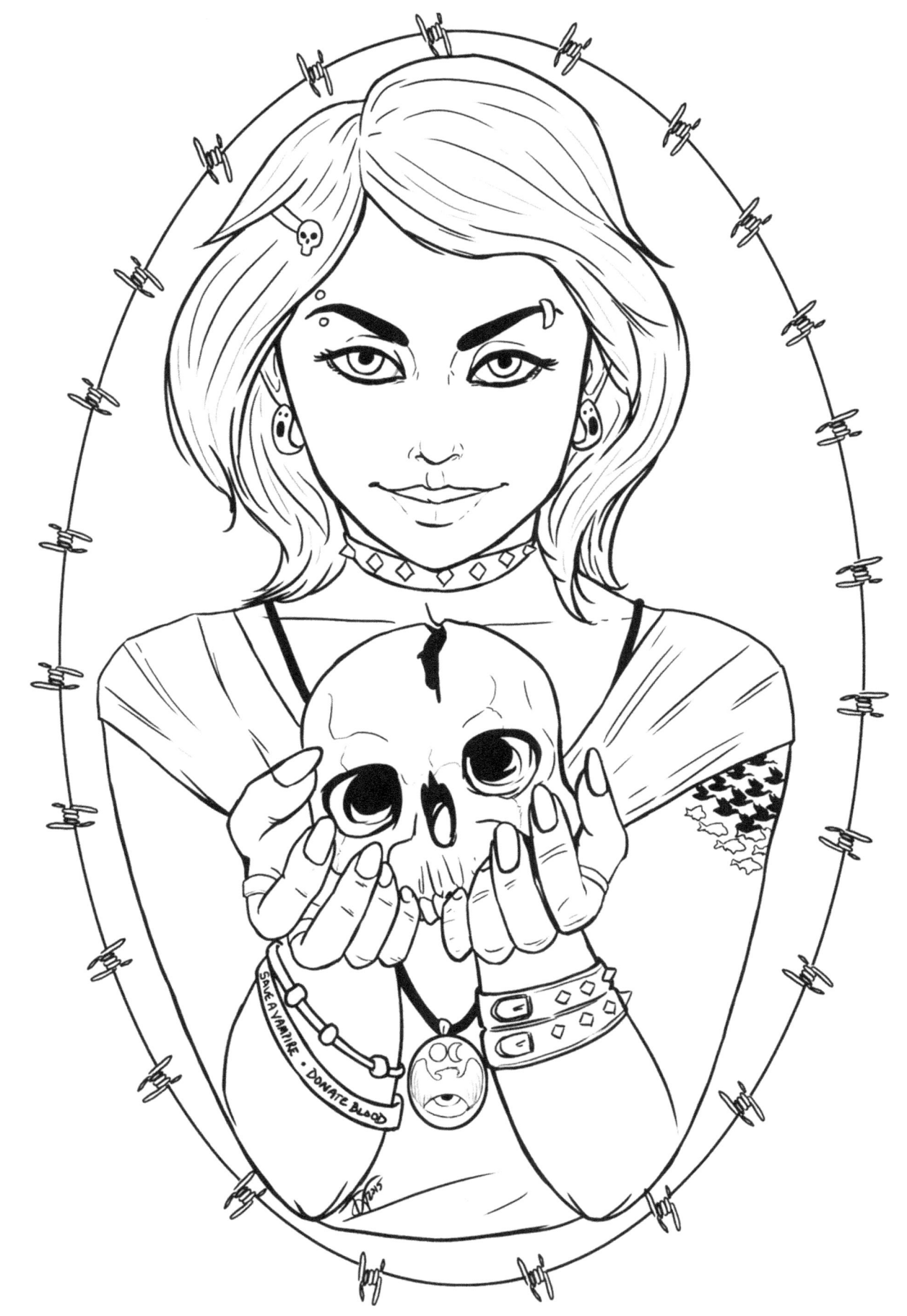

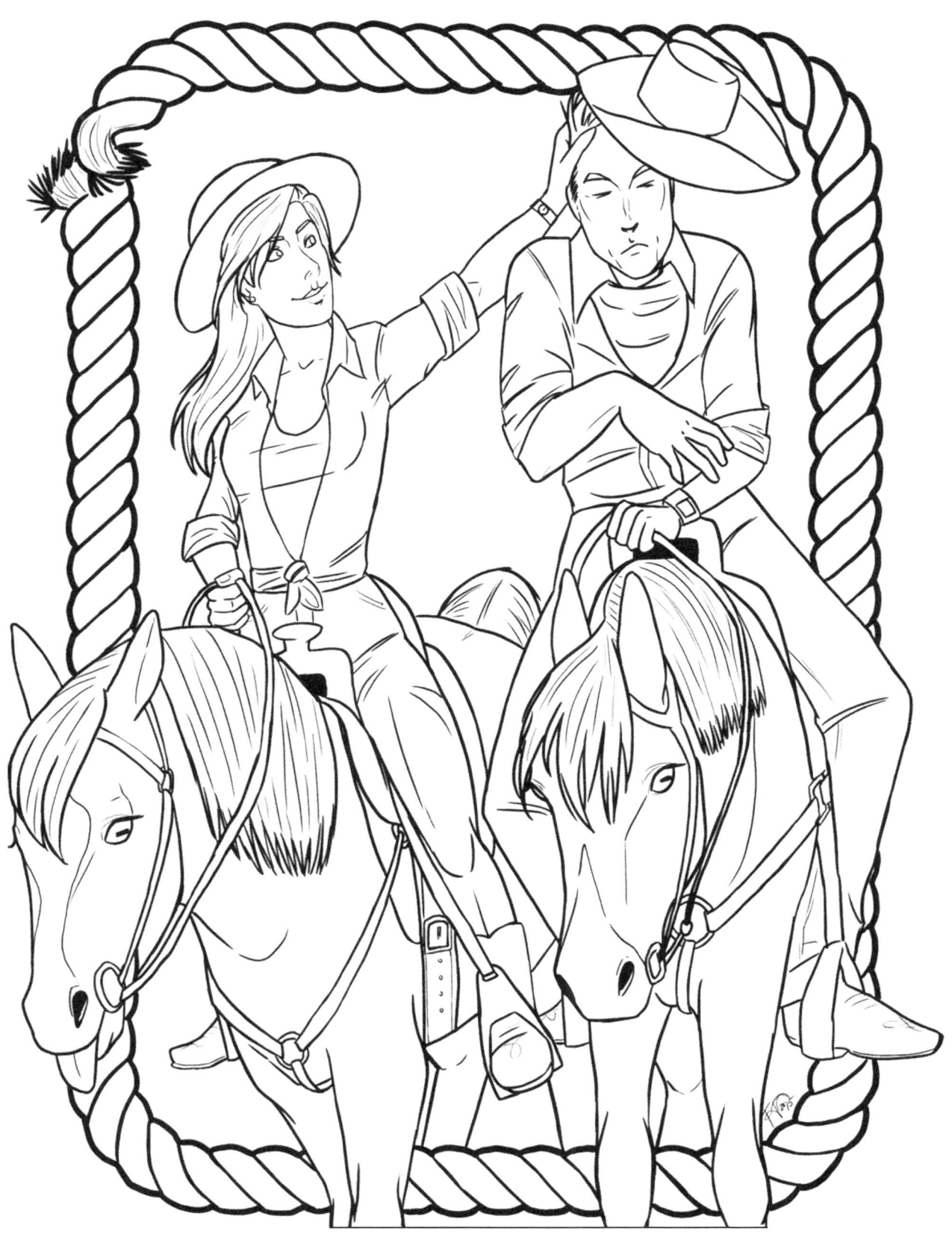

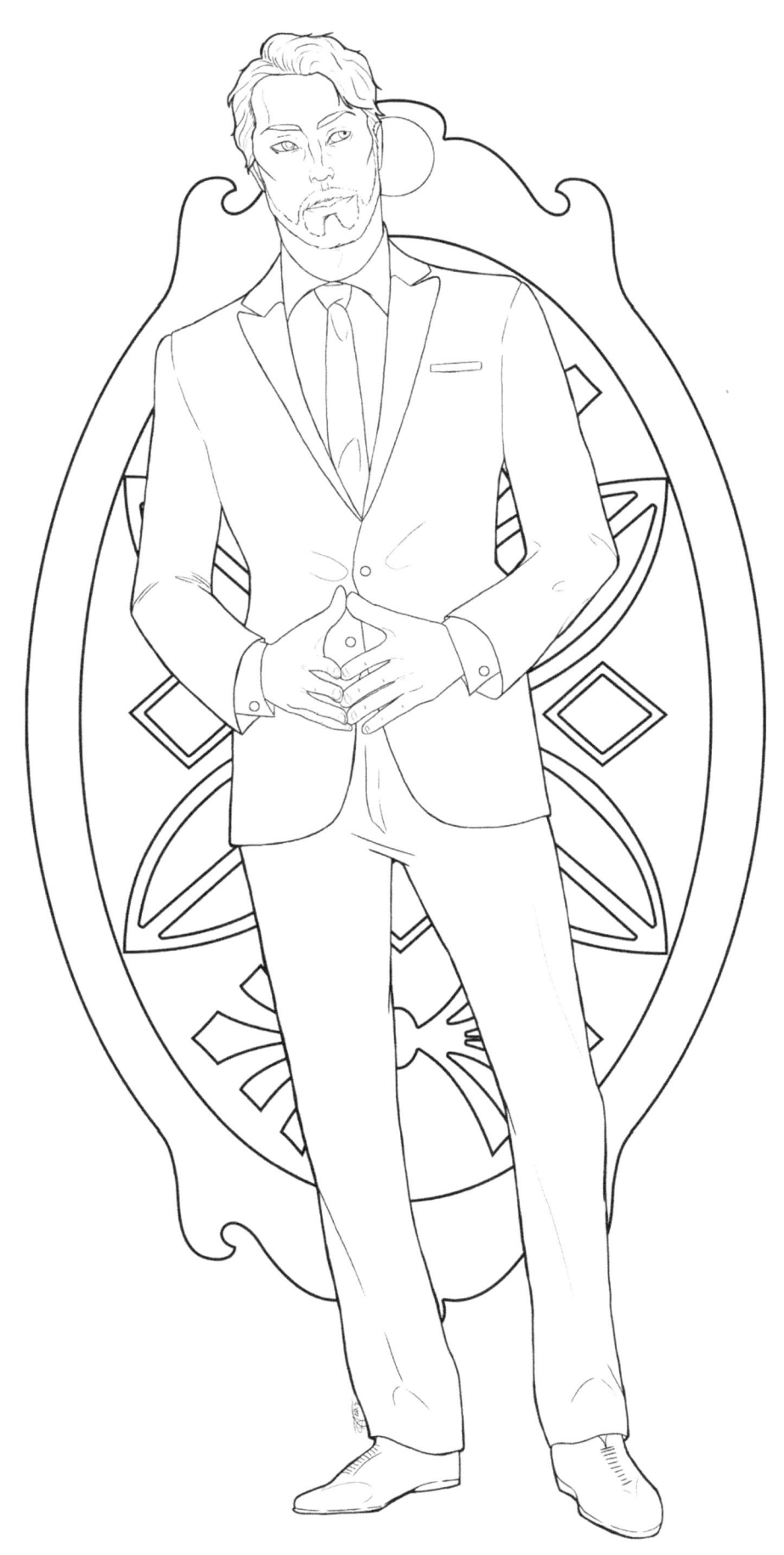

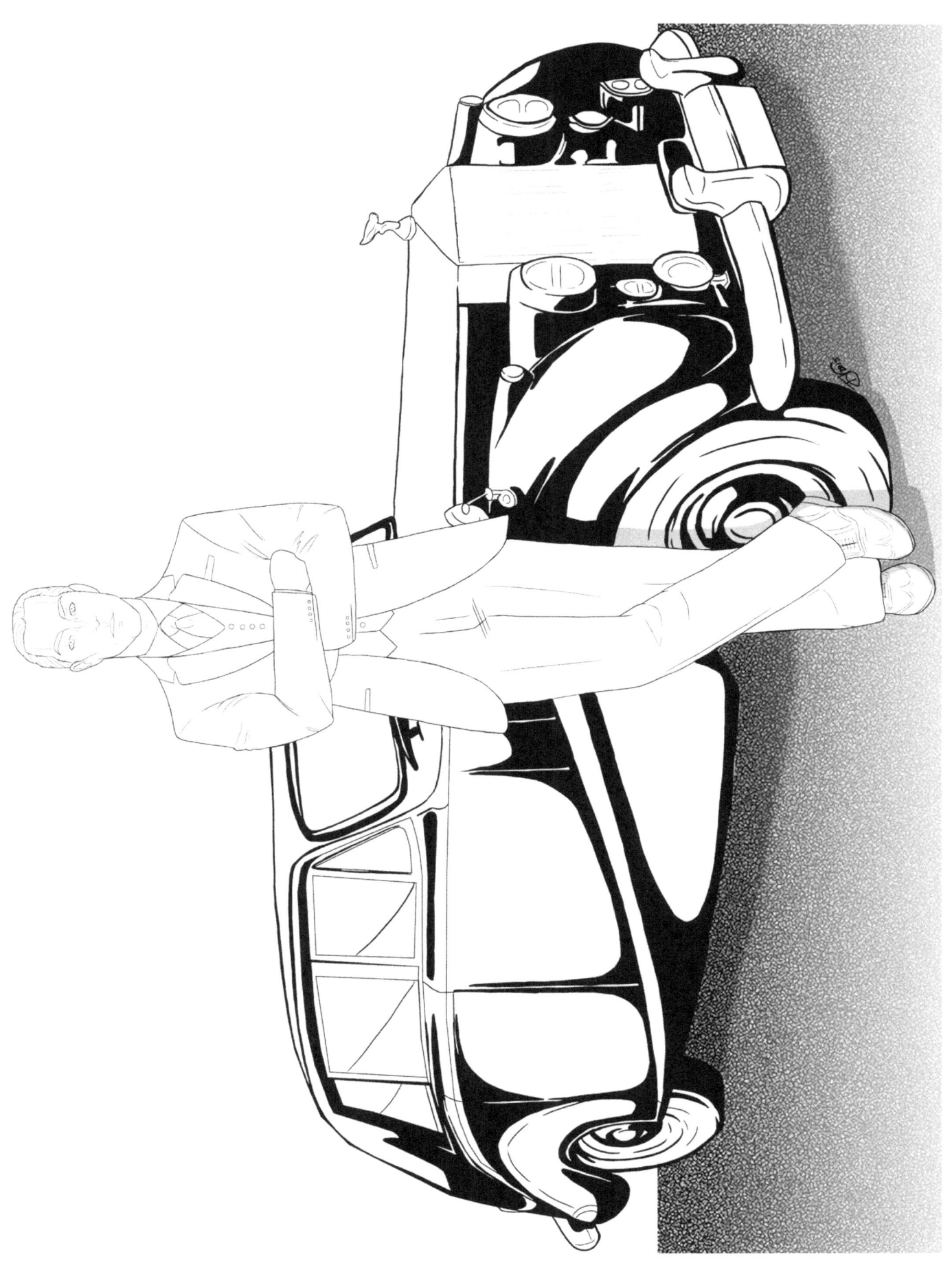

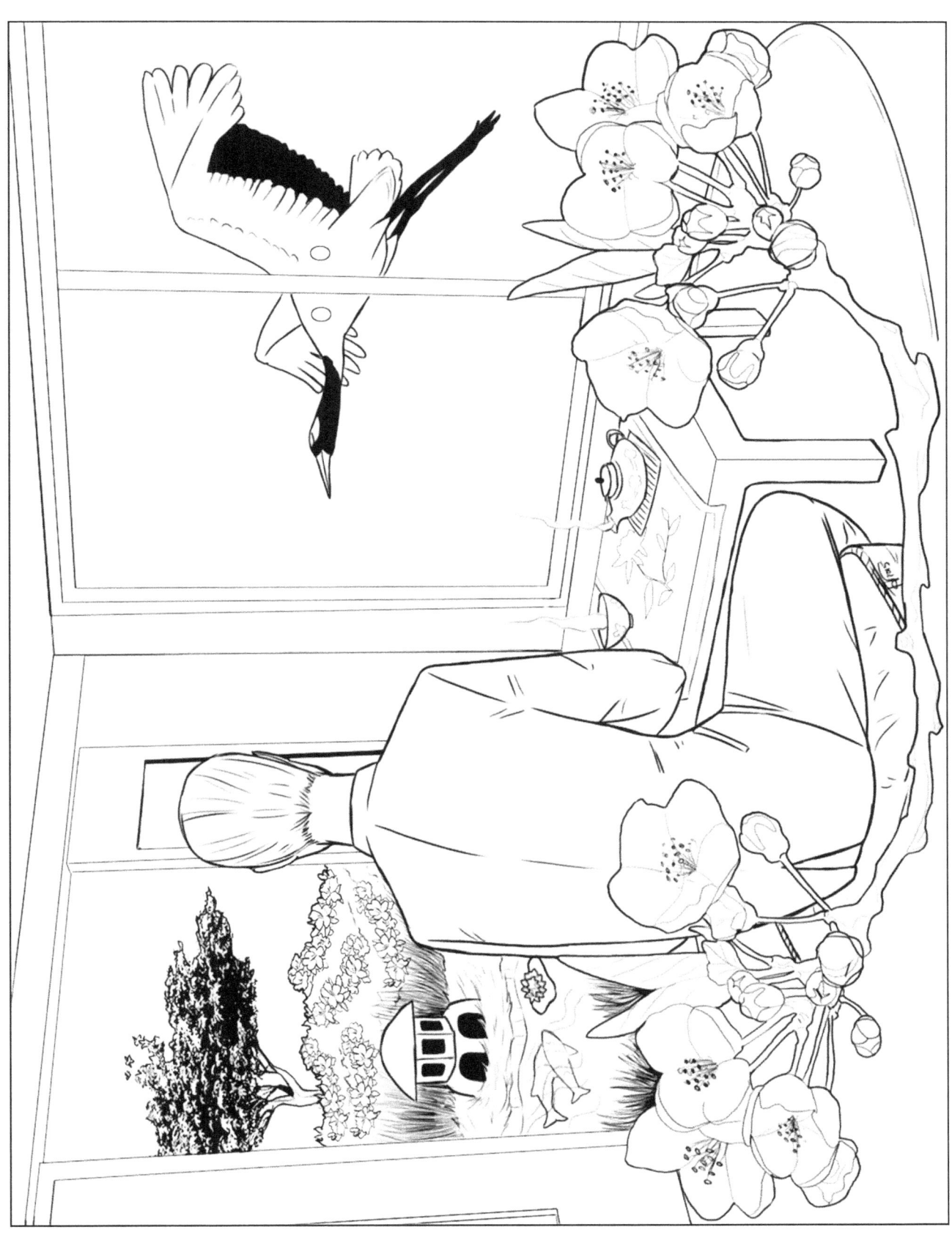

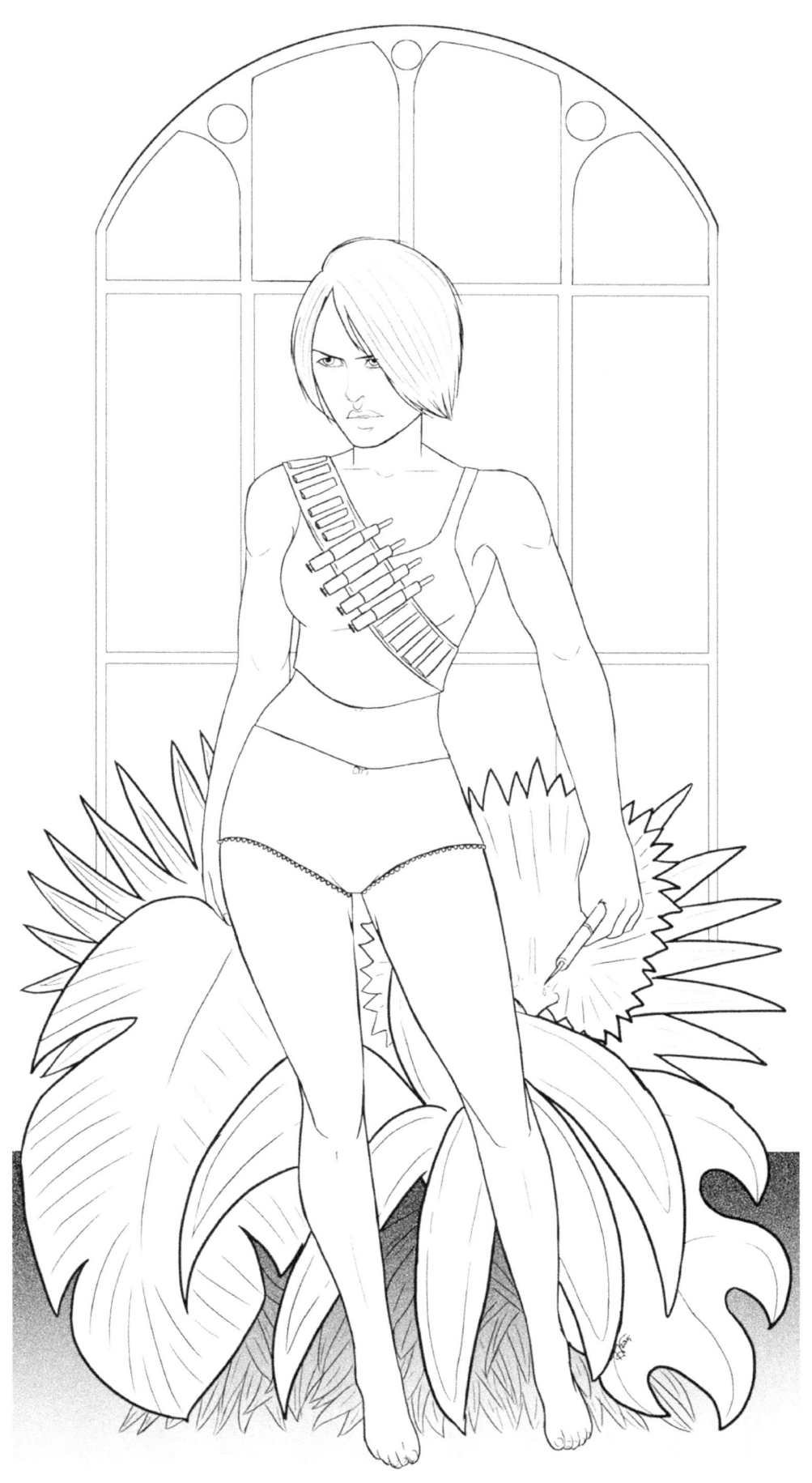

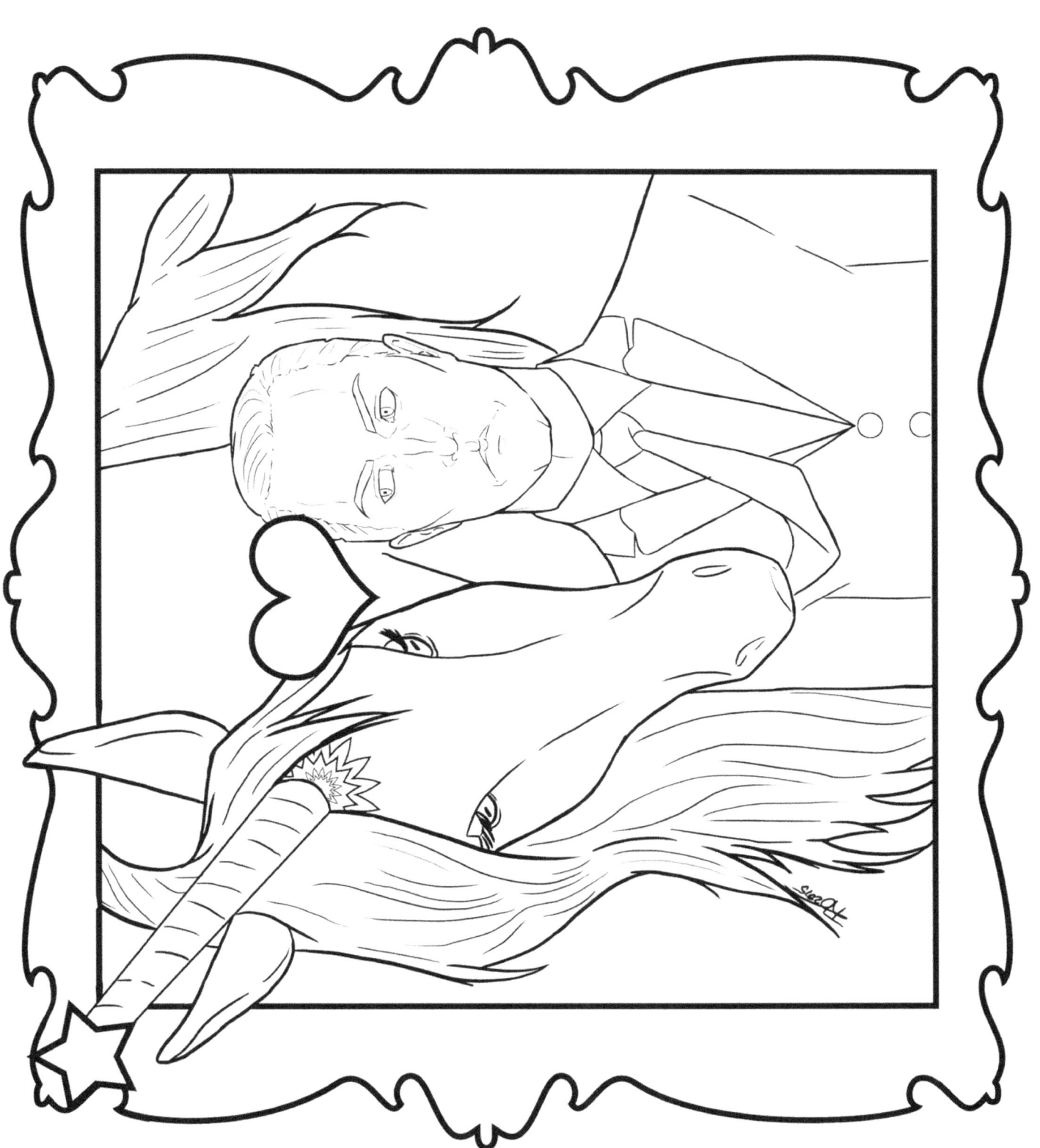

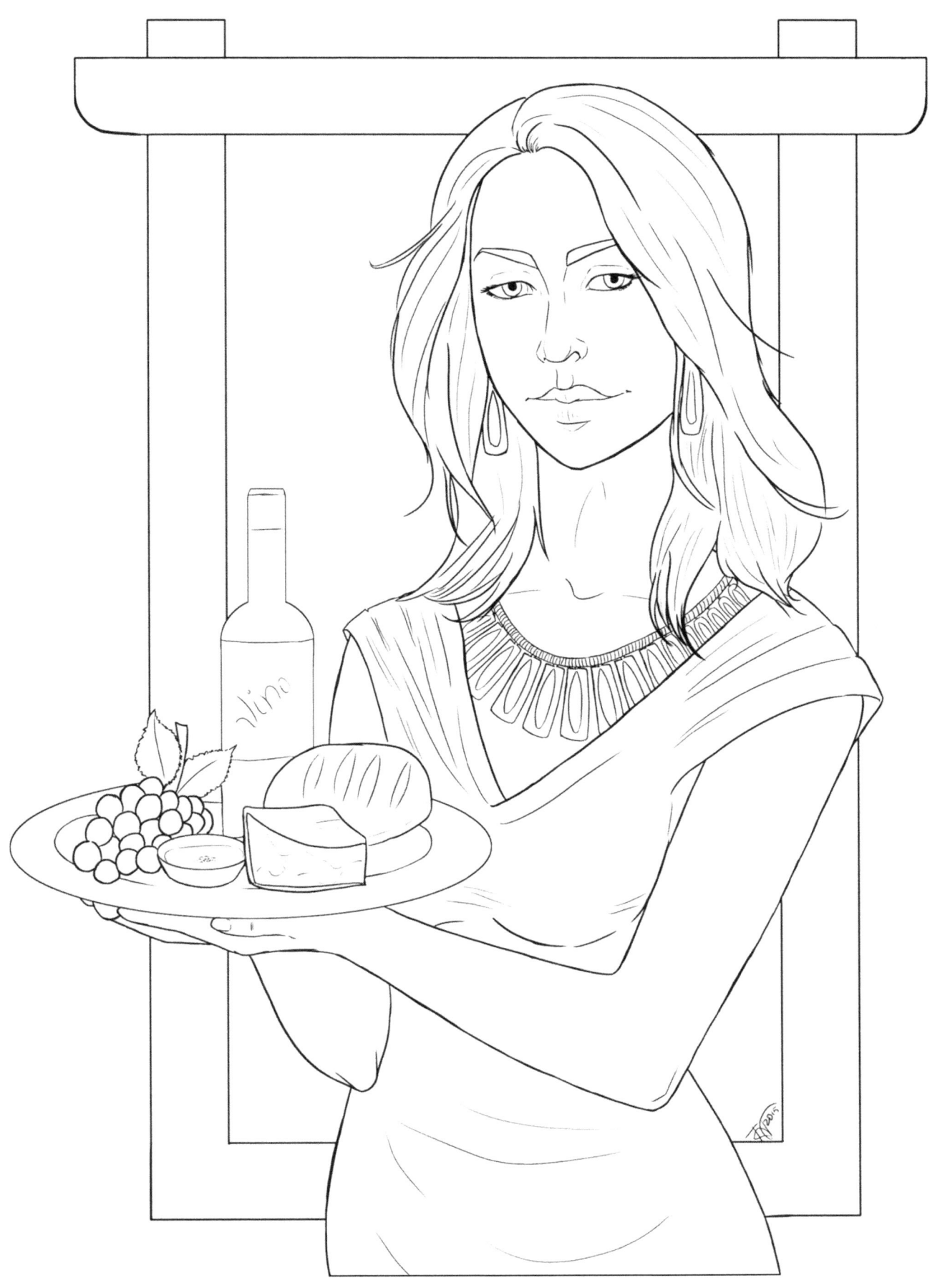

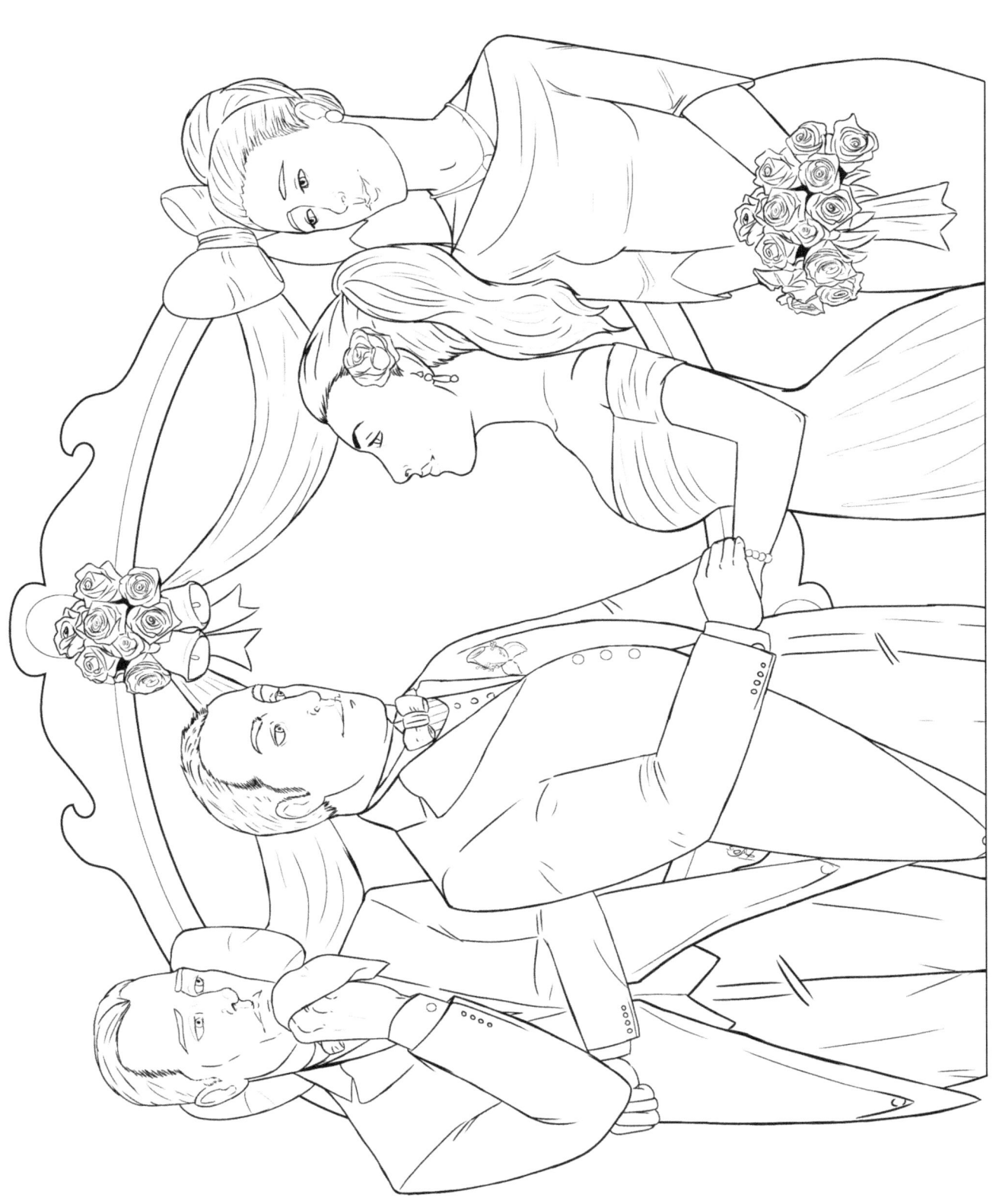

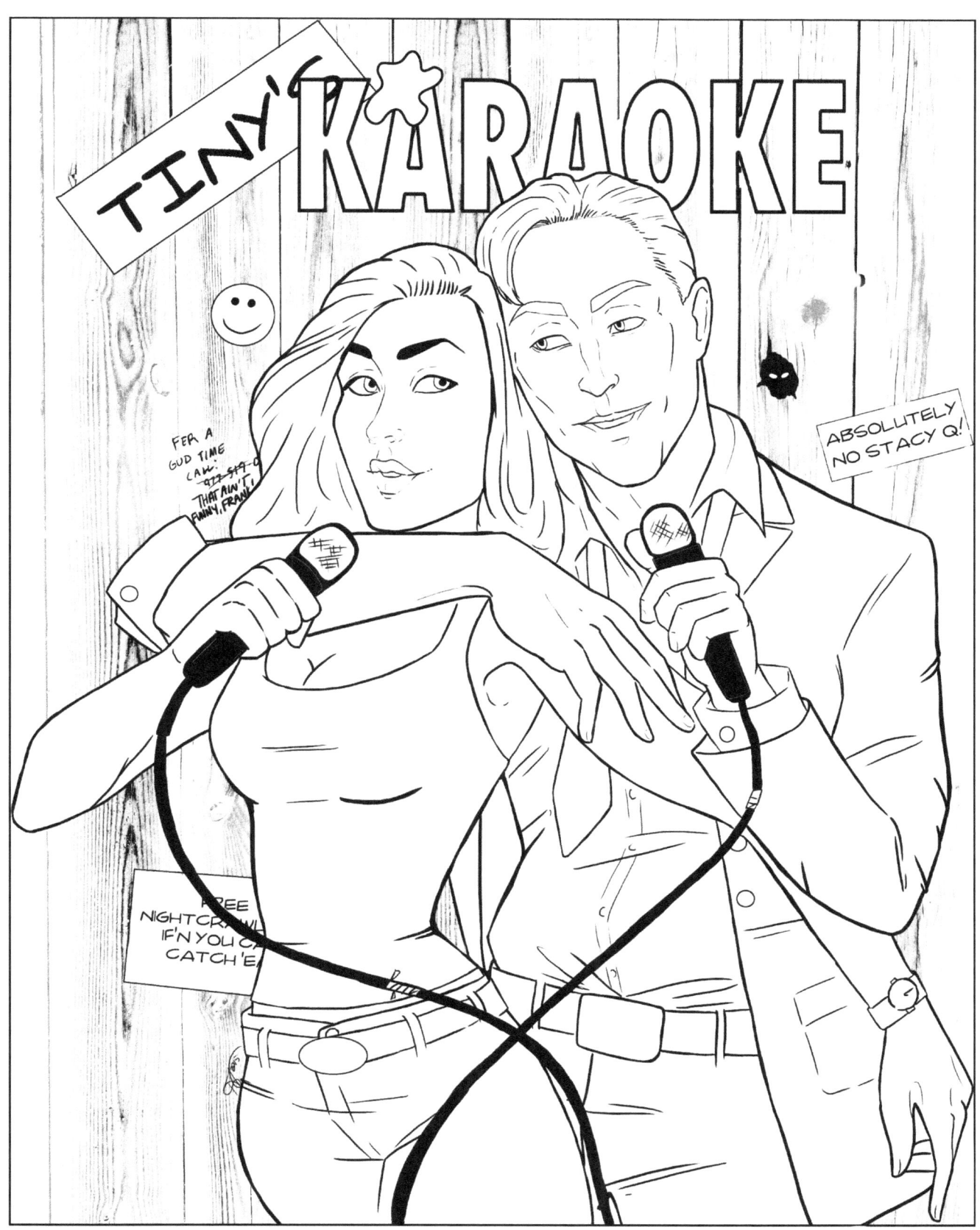

Acknowledgements

This coloring book would not have been possible without the blessing and encouragement from the two men whose books inspired its creation, Douglas Preston and Lincoln Child.

Many tight hugs and thanks to my Bad Habit Support Group; you know who you are. Much love and gratitude to Pamela, who gave me the courage to start this project in the first place, and gave me great ideas. A huge shout out to my excellent group of Pendergast friends here in the States and beyond, you guys motivate and inspire me; to everyone in the "Den" - you know who you are; to many more friends I've made over the past few years: you're more than a girl could hope for.

This wouldn't be a proper Acknowledgements page if I didn't thank my original fans, Mom and Pop. Special thanks to my husband for being a supportive voice and a great curator; also thanks to my son for going to bed early so I could work on these designs; to Casey who got me started on the Pendergast series in the first place; to my family; and to my high school art teacher, Dee, for encouraging me to draw what I feel, and not just what I see.